·My·First·
Encyclopedia

D1509770

Library of Congress Cataloging-in-Publication Data

Snow, Alan.
    My first encyclopedia / illustrated by Alan Snow.
        p.   cm.
    ISBN 0-8167-2519-5 (lib. bdg.)   ISBN 0-8167-2520-9 (pbk.)
    1. Children's encyclopedias and dictionaries. I. Title.
AG6.S6   1992
031-dc20   91-24320

Published by Troll Associates.
Copyright © 1992 Joshua Morris Publishing Inc.
and Alan Snow.
Illustrations © 1991 Alan Snow.
Text by Times Four Publishing Ltd.
All rights reserved.
Printed in Singapore.
10 9 8 7 6 5 4 3 2 1

·My·First·
Encyclopedia

Illustrated by
Alan
Snow

Troll Associates

Contents

What is an Encyclopedia?

How can you find a wide range of information quickly and easily? That was the question facing readers hundreds of years ago. They often knew where to find the answers to their questions in separate books and papers. But that took a lot of time, especially when the needed books and papers were scattered all over the world.

The need for a handy, single source of information led to the creation of the *encyclopedia* (en-SIGH-kluh-PEA-DEE-uh). The word comes from Greek words meaning "general or well-rounded education." An encyclopedia is a book or series of books giving information about different subjects or a lot of information about one subject.

Aristotle, a famous Greek thinker and teacher, is often thought of as the father of the encyclopedia. He lived over 2,000 years ago. During his life, he tried to write down all the knowledge that he had into a series of books.

Today, encyclopedias are made with the help of computers and high-speed printing presses. But the goal is still the same as it was in Aristotle's time—to create one convenient book source of different facts about people, places, ideas, events, and things.

Your body

Your body has many different parts. On the outside you have skin and hair. Inside you have a bony frame and important organs, such as the brain, lungs, heart, and stomach.

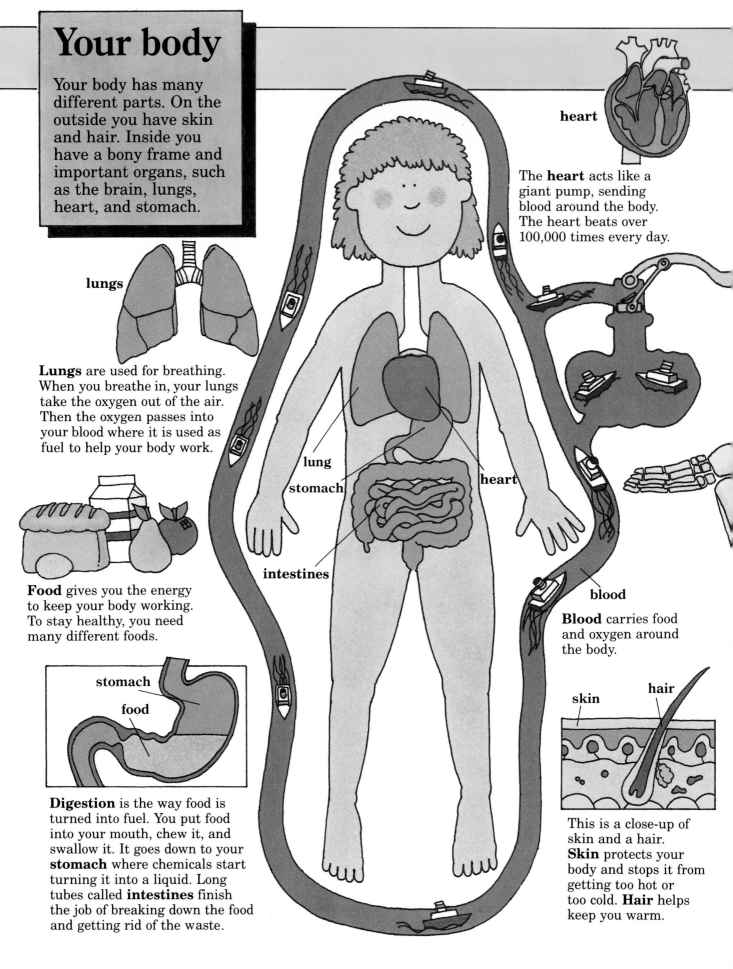

heart

The **heart** acts like a giant pump, sending blood around the body. The heart beats over 100,000 times every day.

lungs

Lungs are used for breathing. When you breathe in, your lungs take the oxygen out of the air. Then the oxygen passes into your blood where it is used as fuel to help your body work.

Food gives you the energy to keep your body working. To stay healthy, you need many different foods.

lung

stomach

heart

intestines

blood

Blood carries food and oxygen around the body.

stomach

food

Digestion is the way food is turned into fuel. You put food into your mouth, chew it, and swallow it. It goes down to your **stomach** where chemicals start turning it into a liquid. Long tubes called **intestines** finish the job of breaking down the food and getting rid of the waste.

skin

hair

This is a close-up of skin and a hair. **Skin** protects your body and stops it from getting too hot or too cold. **Hair** helps keep you warm.

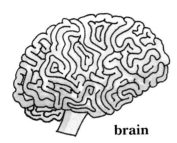

brain

Your **brain,** inside your head, is like a very smart computer. It tells the rest of your body what to do. Your brain sends and receives messages all the time. They travel along the **nerves** that branch through your body.

When you **think,** you use your brain. When you want to **move,** your brain tells your muscles what to do.

When you **remember** something, the memory is stored in your brain. And your brain makes sure you breathe even when you are asleep!

Thinking

Moving

Remembering

skull

elbow

Babies have over 300 bones but adults have only about 206! Some bones join together when you grow.

The **skeleton,** which includes your ribs, is the bony frame inside your body. It protects important things such as the brain and heart.

ribs

Joints are the places where your bones meet. Your **knee** is a joint.

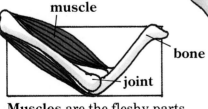

muscle

bone

knee

joint

Muscles are the fleshy parts that cover your bones. They stretch and shrink like elastic to make your body move.

You have five **senses.** You hear with your ears, see with your eyes, smell with your nose, touch with your skin, and taste with your tongue.

sight

smell

taste

hearing

touch

People of the world

Every day, the number of people in the world goes up by about 223,285. That's almost 155 people *per minute!* Some live in tiny villages. Others live in huge cities.

Long ago

Here are some facts you may not know about people who lived thousands of years ago.

4,500 years ago: The Egyptians buried their kings in huge stone pyramids.

2,500 years ago: The ancient Greeks built beautiful buildings.

2,000 years ago: The Romans ruled Europe. Romans liked chariot racing.

No two people in the world look exactly alike. Skin can be light or dark. Hair can be black, brown, blond, or red. Some people are tall. Some are short.

The peoples of the world speak thousands of different **languages.** More people speak Chinese than any other language. Babies copy the sounds they hear around them, so they learn the language of their own family.

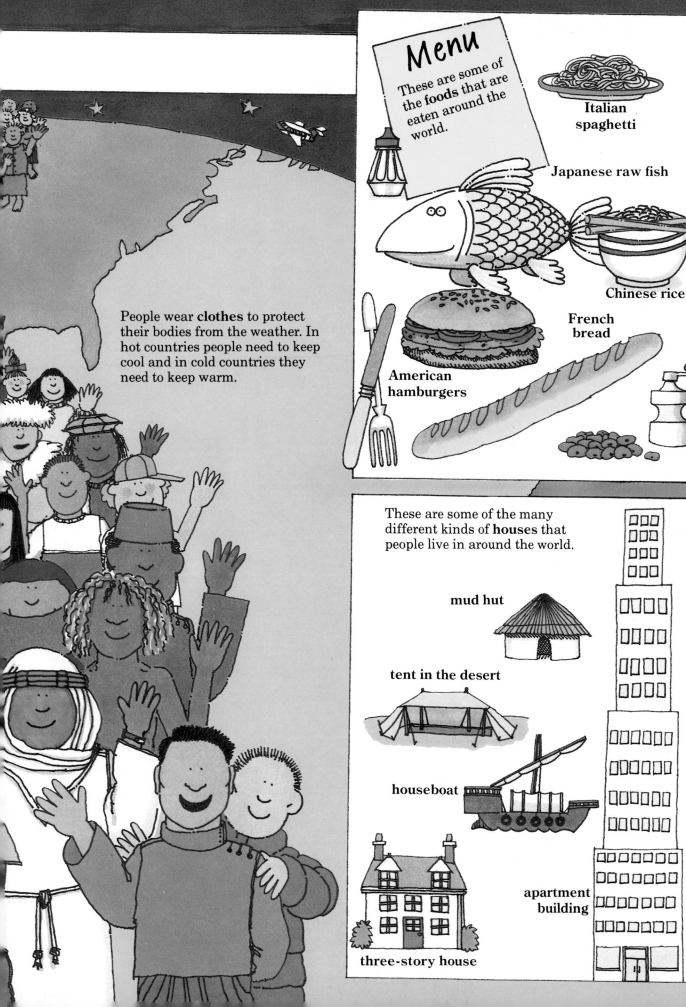

People wear **clothes** to protect their bodies from the weather. In hot countries people need to keep cool and in cold countries they need to keep warm.

Menu

These are some of the **foods** that are eaten around the world.

Italian spaghetti

Japanese raw fish

Chinese rice

French bread

American hamburgers

These are some of the many different kinds of **houses** that people live in around the world.

mud hut

tent in the desert

houseboat

apartment building

three-story house

Keeping in touch

You can send messages to other people in many different ways—by talking, writing, or using machines. These are all forms of **communication**.

Our earliest ancestors invented **languages** and drew **picture messages**.

cave dwellers

Egyptian writing

Ancient Egyptians wrote using this **picture language**.

Writing was one way people sent messages to each other. But they also needed ways of sending messages more quickly.

Some people in the Alps mountains in Switzerland used to send **sound messages** to each other using huge horns called alpenhorns.

Some American Indians used to send **smoke signal messages**.

alpenhorns

smoke signal

semaphore

Codes were invented for sending messages. Codes use special words, letters, and signs.

Semaphore is a code using flags. You spell out each letter by holding the flags in a special way. These pictures show you a semaphore alphabet. Can you spell your name in flags?

Morse code uses dot (•) and dash (—) sounds for the letters of the alphabet. The sounds are tapped into a machine that sends electrical messages.

Can you crack this International Morse code message?

A	• —	N	— •
B	— • • •	O	— — —
C	— • — •	P	• — — •
D	— • •	Q	— — • —
E	•	R	• — •
F	• • — •	S	• • •
G	— — •	T	—
H	• • • •	U	• • —
I	• •	V	• • • —
J	• — — —	W	• — —
K	— • —	X	— • • —
L	• — • •	Y	— • — —
M	— —	Z	— — • •

International Morse code

Modern technology has given us new machines for communicating with each other. Pictures, sounds, and writing can be sent across the world in just a few seconds.

fax machine

Fax machines copy and send words and pictures by telephone.

computer

Computers store lots of information. Some can send each other messages.

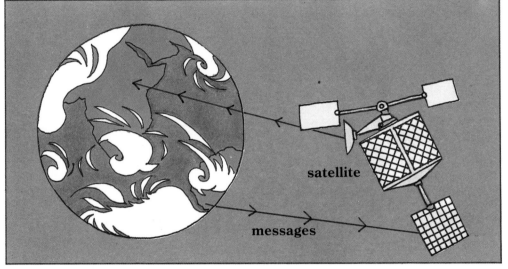

satellite

messages

Communication satellites in space can send both sounds and pictures. Messages are beamed up to these satellites, which then bounce them back to other areas of the world.

Radio stations and television (TV) stations send electrical signals through the air. Your **radio** picks up radio signals and turns them into sounds. Your **TV** picks up TV signals and turns them into sounds and pictures.

Videotapes store sounds and pictures on tape. You can watch movies on TV by using a videocassette recorder (VCR) or player.

radio

Listen to my favorite song!

I just read a great book.

book

Writing is an important way of communicating. **Books and magazines** are fun to read. **Newspapers** tell you what is going on.

television

videocassette

Let's watch a movie.

VCR

It's nice to hear from you.

Telephones pick up your voice and send it to the telephone number you called. It's a good way for friends, families, and businesses to send messages.

telephone

Transportation

Two hundred years ago, the fastest you could travel was by horse or sailboat. Today there are so many ways of traveling—on land, in the air, and by sea. How many of these vehicles have you traveled in?

Cars are the most popular kind of transportation. Most cars have engines that burn gasoline. As it burns, it makes pistons go up and down. The movement of the pistons makes the wheels go around.

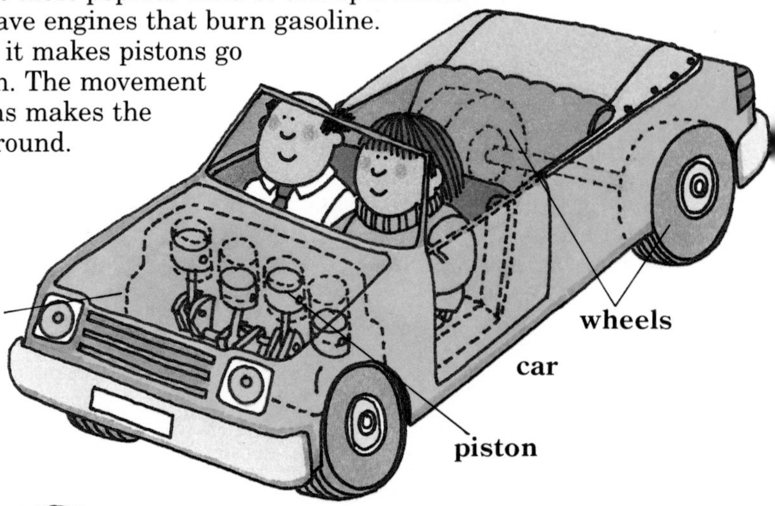

engine

wheels

car

piston

Trucks carry large loads. The heaviest truckload ever carried weighed about the same as 54 male African elephants!

trucks

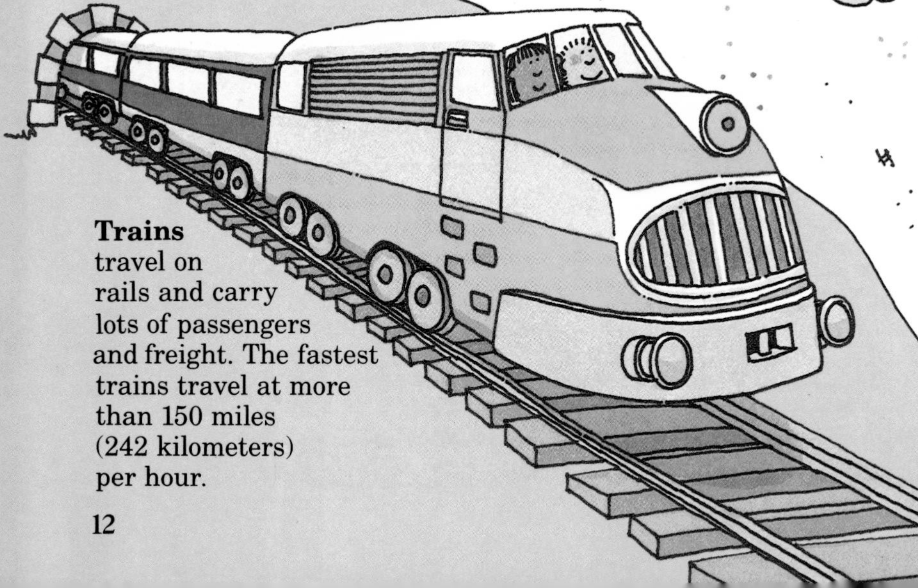

train

Trains travel on rails and carry lots of passengers and freight. The fastest trains travel at more than 150 miles (242 kilometers) per hour.

motorcycle

Motorcycles have two wheels and an engine. Some motorcycles travel very fast.

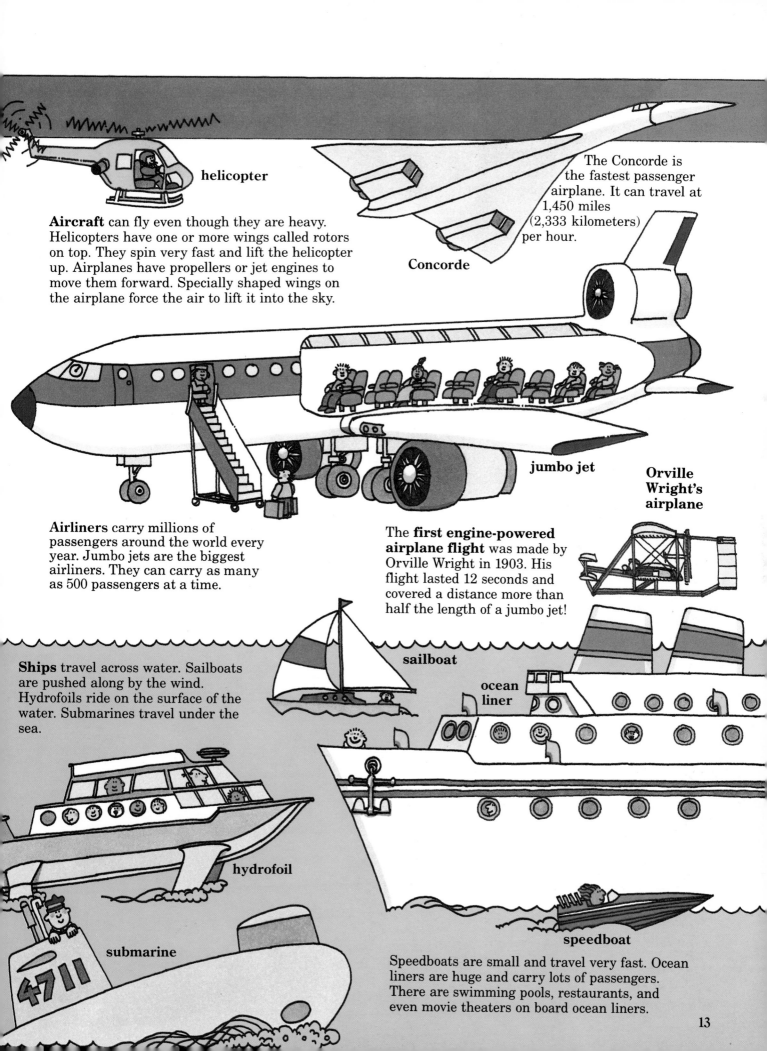

helicopter

Aircraft can fly even though they are heavy. Helicopters have one or more wings called rotors on top. They spin very fast and lift the helicopter up. Airplanes have propellers or jet engines to move them forward. Specially shaped wings on the airplane force the air to lift it into the sky.

The Concorde is the fastest passenger airplane. It can travel at 1,450 miles (2,333 kilometers) per hour.

Concorde

jumbo jet

Orville Wright's airplane

Airliners carry millions of passengers around the world every year. Jumbo jets are the biggest airliners. They can carry as many as 500 passengers at a time.

The **first engine-powered airplane flight** was made by Orville Wright in 1903. His flight lasted 12 seconds and covered a distance more than half the length of a jumbo jet!

sailboat

ocean liner

Ships travel across water. Sailboats are pushed along by the wind. Hydrofoils ride on the surface of the water. Submarines travel under the sea.

hydrofoil

submarine

speedboat

Speedboats are small and travel very fast. Ocean liners are huge and carry lots of passengers. There are swimming pools, restaurants, and even movie theaters on board ocean liners.

13

Prehistoric world

Dinosaurs and other prehistoric creatures lived long before there were people. Dinosaurs ruled the Earth for about 140 million years. They all died out millions of years ago.

Pteranodon
27-foot (8-meter) wingspan
Pteranodon was a flying reptile. It had leathery wings but could not fly very well.

Diplodocus
90 feet (27 meters) long

The **biggest dinosaurs** were twice the length of a tennis court. They were plant-eaters with huge, heavy bodies and very long necks.

Diplodocus was one of the larger dinosaurs. It was a plant-eater.

Triceratops had three horns, and a shield of bone around its neck. It was very strong.

Tyrannosaurus
50 feet (15 meters) long

Tyrannosaurus was the largest meat-eater. It was very fierce. It might have caught other dinosaurs and killed them with its sharp teeth.

Triceratops 30 feet (9 meters) long.

The **smallest dinosaurs** were the size of chickens. They ate insects and ran fast on their back legs.

Fossils (see below) are the remains of ancient plants and animals left behind in rocks. They help show us what prehistoric creatures looked like.

Dinosaurs were reptiles. Their babies hatched out of eggs.

Compsognathus
2 feet (½ meter) long

baby dinosaur

Animals today

Millions of animals live on Earth. Some live on the land. Some swim in the seas and rivers. Others fly in the air. Here and on the next two pages you can see some of the many kinds of animals living today.

ants

All **insects** have six legs. Bees, butterflies, and beetles are insects. They have wings and can fly. Beetles' wings are folded away when they are not flying. Some insects, such as worker ants, cannot fly.

butterfly

bee

Spiders are small animals with eight legs. Some spiders spin webs of sticky thread. They eat any insects that get caught in their web.

spider

There are about 300,000 different kinds of beetles!

beetle

shark

angelfish

Amphibians are animals that can live on land and in water. Frogs are amphibians. They lay their eggs in water. Tadpoles hatch out of the eggs and swim in the water. Then they grow legs and climb onto the land. At last, they turn into frogs.

eggs

tadpole without legs

tadpole with legs

Millions of **fish** live in seas, rivers, and lakes. They can breathe underwater. Some live in large groups called schools. Sharks are meat-eating fish with sharp teeth.

octopus

school of fish

shell

There are many strange **sea creatures.** Octopuses have eight arms with suckers on them. Some sea creatures, such as lobsters, have soft bodies inside hard shells. There are sea creatures living even in the deep, cold seas.

lobster

More animals

bat

monkey

giraffe

Mammals are warm-blooded animals. Their bodies are covered with hair or fur to keep them warm. Mammal mothers produce milk for their babies to drink. There are many different kinds of mammals. Whales and dolphins are mammals that live in the sea. Giraffes, monkeys, horses, dogs, and bats are all mammals. You are a mammal, too!

human

horse

dolphin

dog

whale

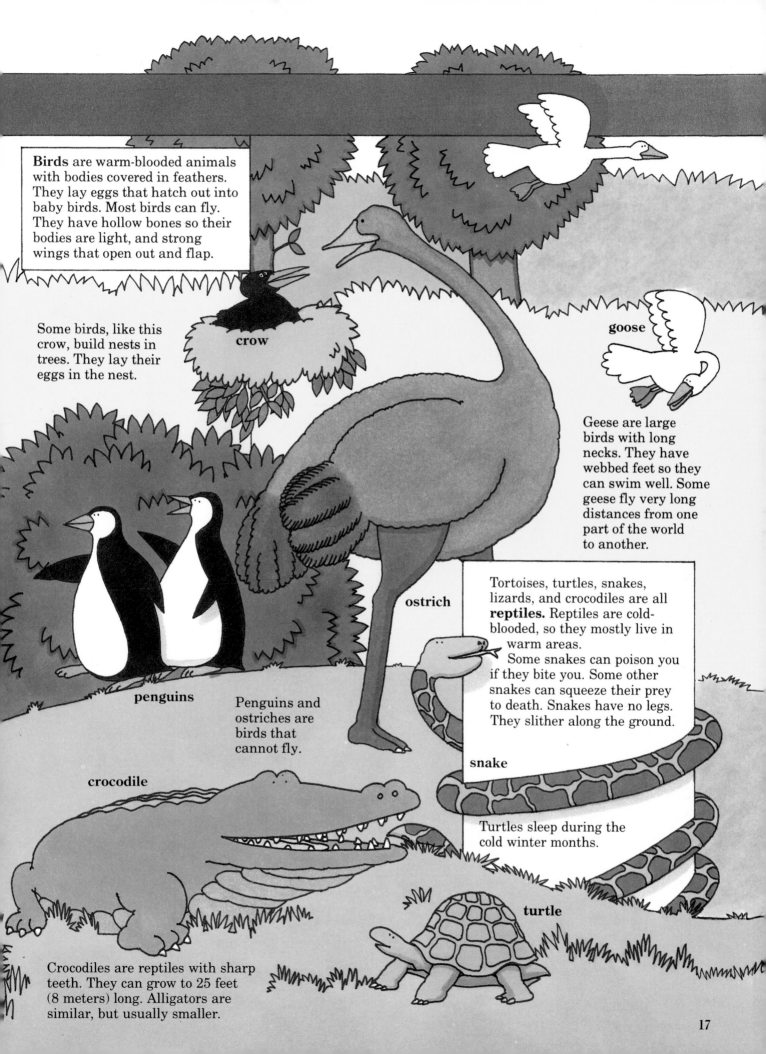

Birds are warm-blooded animals with bodies covered in feathers. They lay eggs that hatch out into baby birds. Most birds can fly. They have hollow bones so their bodies are light, and strong wings that open out and flap.

Some birds, like this crow, build nests in trees. They lay their eggs in the nest.

crow

goose

Geese are large birds with long necks. They have webbed feet so they can swim well. Some geese fly very long distances from one part of the world to another.

ostrich

penguins

Penguins and ostriches are birds that cannot fly.

Tortoises, turtles, snakes, lizards, and crocodiles are all **reptiles.** Reptiles are cold-blooded, so they mostly live in warm areas.
Some snakes can poison you if they bite you. Some other snakes can squeeze their prey to death. Snakes have no legs. They slither along the ground.

snake

Turtles sleep during the cold winter months.

crocodile

turtle

Crocodiles are reptiles with sharp teeth. They can grow to 25 feet (8 meters) long. Alligators are similar, but usually smaller.

Plants

Any living thing that is not an animal is a **plant.** Plants grow all over the Earth, even on mountains and in deserts. Plants are very important because they release a gas called oxygen, which people and other animals need to breathe.

toucan

Plants provide food and homes for many animals. Butterflies, monkeys, and birds all depend on plants in some way.

hummingbird

monkey

In some countries there are hot, steamy **rain forests,** where millions of plants live. Many wild animals make their homes there. Rain forest plants give out lots of oxygen and help to keep the air clean. It is important to stop people from cutting down too much of the forests.

Some chemicals from air pollution mix with water in clouds. This can cause **acid rain,** which is harmful to trees and animals.

Trees are very large plants. The largest living things in the world are trees called **sequoias.** They grow in California and Oregon.

The biggest sequoia of all is about 2,500 years old and 275 feet (84 meters) tall. That's as tall as 48 men standing on each other's shoulders!

If you cut the tree up, it would make 5 *billion* (5,000,000,000) matchsticks!

sequoia

What do plants eat?

Most plants make their own food, using air, sunlight, water, and soil.

Roots draw up water and minerals from the soil. Leaves take in air and light. Plants die if they cannot get light and water.

leaf
roots
soil

Many **farmers** grow plants for people to eat. These farmers are growing **wheat** in huge, flat fields. When the wheat is ripe, a machine called a combine harvester cuts it and takes out the wheat seeds. The seeds are taken to a mill where they are ground up into a powder called flour. Flour is an important food. It is used to make bread, pasta, and cookies.

farm

wheat

combine harvester

wheat seeds

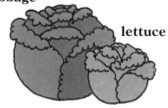

We eat many different plants.

Rice and wheat are plant **seeds.**

cabbage

potato

carrot

Potatoes and carrots are plant **roots.**

rice

wheat

lettuce

Lettuce and cabbages are plant **leaves.**

Celery is a plant **stalk.**

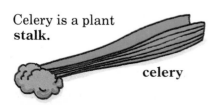

celery

fruit

Fruits are the parts of flowering plants that contain **seeds.** They are usually good to eat.

Earth

The Earth is a ball of mostly rock spinning in space. If you could cut it open, you would find very hot liquid rock deep inside. The center, or core, is probably solid.

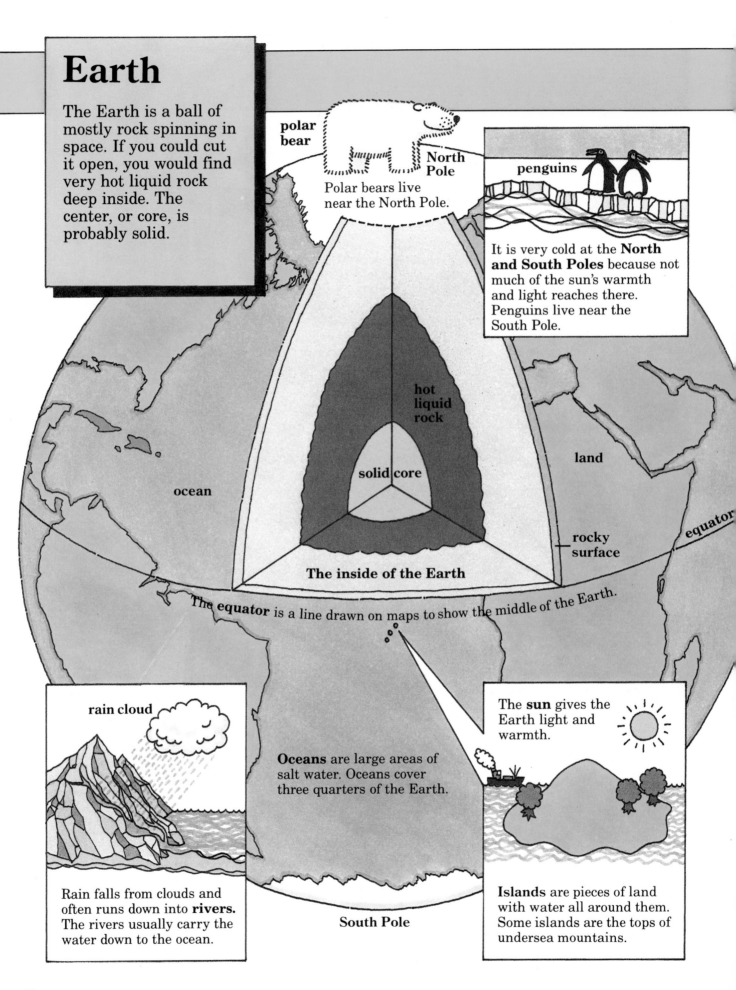

polar bear

North Pole

Polar bears live near the North Pole.

penguins

It is very cold at the **North and South Poles** because not much of the sun's warmth and light reaches there. Penguins live near the South Pole.

hot liquid rock

land

solid core

ocean

rocky surface

equator

The inside of the Earth

The **equator** is a line drawn on maps to show the middle of the Earth.

rain cloud

Rain falls from clouds and often runs down into **rivers.** The rivers usually carry the water down to the ocean.

Oceans are large areas of salt water. Oceans cover three quarters of the Earth.

The **sun** gives the Earth light and warmth.

Islands are pieces of land with water all around them. Some islands are the tops of undersea mountains.

South Pole

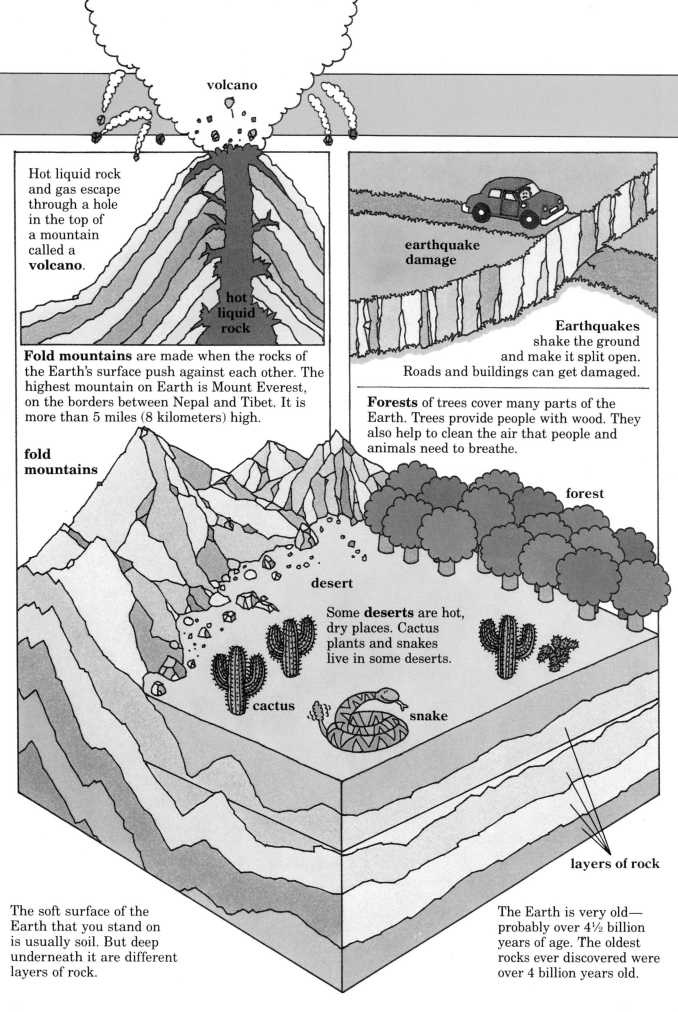

volcano

Hot liquid rock and gas escape through a hole in the top of a mountain called a **volcano**.

hot liquid rock

earthquake damage

Earthquakes shake the ground and make it split open. Roads and buildings can get damaged.

Forests of trees cover many parts of the Earth. Trees provide people with wood. They also help to clean the air that people and animals need to breathe.

forest

Fold mountains are made when the rocks of the Earth's surface push against each other. The highest mountain on Earth is Mount Everest, on the borders between Nepal and Tibet. It is more than 5 miles (8 kilometers) high.

fold mountains

desert

Some **deserts** are hot, dry places. Cactus plants and snakes live in some deserts.

cactus

snake

layers of rock

The soft surface of the Earth that you stand on is usually soil. But deep underneath it are different layers of rock.

The Earth is very old—probably over 4½ billion years of age. The oldest rocks ever discovered were over 4 billion years old.

Space

Space is so big that nobody knows how big it is. Earth is just one small planet among millions of other planets and stars.

The **Earth** travels around the **sun** once each year. It also spins around on its own once each day.

During the day the sun shines on your side of the Earth. It is then night on the other side of the Earth.

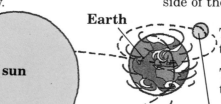

Earth

sun

moon

The Earth goes around the sun.

The **moon** goes around the Earth.

This is what **Earth** looks like from space. You can see some land, but much of Earth is covered by sea. There are clouds swirling around the planet.

space shuttle

The **space shuttle** can carry people and machines into space. Two powerful rockets carry it through the air and into space. When the space shuttle comes back to Earth, it lands just like an airplane.

★ **star**

You can see lots of **stars** shining in the night sky. Each one is a ball of burning gas. The stars are millions of miles away from Earth.

astronaut

satellite

Satellites can help scientists learn more about the Earth and about space. These astronauts are fixing a satellite.

The **sun** is the star nearest to Earth. But it is still many millions of miles away. The sun is very hot. At its core, or center, the sun has a temperature of about 27 *million* degrees Fahrenheit (15 million degrees Celsius).

Nine **planets** move around the sun. Mercury is close to the sun, so it is very hot. Pluto is far away, so it is icy cold.

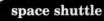

Mercury   Venus   Earth   Mars

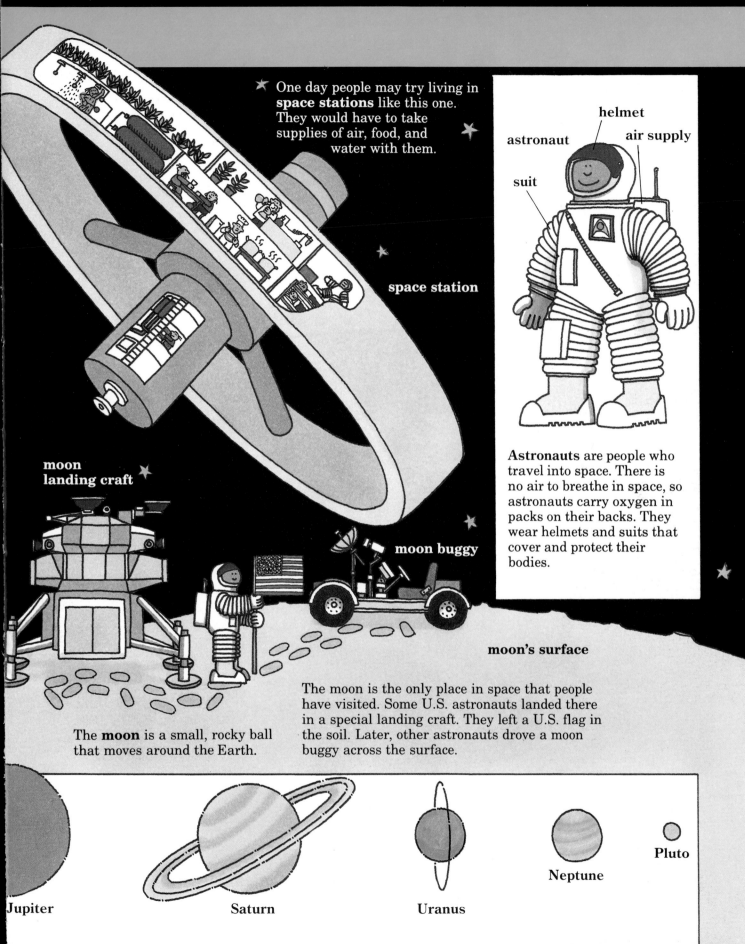

One day people may try living in **space stations** like this one. They would have to take supplies of air, food, and water with them.

space station

helmet

astronaut   air supply

suit

Astronauts are people who travel into space. There is no air to breathe in space, so astronauts carry oxygen in packs on their backs. They wear helmets and suits that cover and protect their bodies.

moon landing craft

moon buggy

moon's surface

The **moon** is a small, rocky ball that moves around the Earth.

The moon is the only place in space that people have visited. Some U.S. astronauts landed there in a special landing craft. They left a U.S. flag in the soil. Later, other astronauts drove a moon buggy across the surface.

Jupiter

Saturn

Uranus

Neptune

Pluto

It's the greatest...

These are some of the tallest, fastest, and biggest people and things in the world.

spacecraft

Tallest office building:
Sears Tower, Chicago.
1,454 feet (443 meters) high. It has 110 stories and 16,000 windows. Almost 17,000 people work there.

These are some of the **fastest speeds** people have reached:

swimming	5 mph (8 kph)
roller skating	27 mph (43 kph)
running	27 mph (44 kph)
skateboarding	53 mph (85 kph)
bicycling	65 mph (105 kph)
skiing	139 mph (224 kph)
in a speedboat	178 mph (286 kph)
in a jet- engined car	633 mph (1,019 kph)
in a spacecraft	24,791 mph (39,889 kph)

mph = miles per hour
kph = kilometers per hour

skateboarder

Tallest man:
Robert Pershing Wadlow, from Illinois (lived 1918-1940). 8 feet 11.1 inches (2.7 meters) tall.

Tallest woman:
Zeng Jinlian, from China (lived 1964-1982). 8 feet 1.75 inches (2½ meters) tall.

These are the speeds some animals can travel at:

snail	rabbit	cheetah	spinetail swift
0.03 mph (0.05 kph)	45 mph (72 kph)	63 mph (101 kph)	106 mph (171 kph)

pizza

The **biggest pizza** ever made was 111 feet (34 meters) across. That's over twice as wide as a basketball court!

The **biggest ice-cream sundae** ever made weighed 54,915 pounds (24,909 kilograms).

The **largest hamburger** ever made weighed 5,520 pounds (2,504 kilograms).

The **biggest sausage** ever made was 13 miles (21 kilometers) long. That is as long as the island of Manhattan in New York!

Sears Tower

sausage

Hop a houseboat,
helicopter, or hydrofoil
to some great
Encyclopedia fun
on the next page...

Wheels of Fortune

On a blank piece of paper, write down all four names of the wheeled vehicles shown here. Now pretend that one of the wheeled vehicles is carrying a lot of money inside it. But which wheeled vehicle is it? Crack the International Morse code message here to get your only clue to the name of this vehicle. Write the clue out on the same piece of paper. Now do you know which vehicle has the money?

..-/- ..-/... ---/..-/- ---/...- -/..../../..-/... ---/---/..-/.-../-

Play by the Numbers

Are you good at remembering numbers? Here's a way to find out. Use a separate piece of paper and a pencil to jot down letters **a** through **f**. Next to each letter there, write the number that would correctly fill in the blank of each sentence below.

A. Spiders have __ legs.
B. Triceratops had __ horns.
C. The first engine-powered airplane flight lasted __ seconds.
D. You have __ senses.
E. Moving around the sun are __ planets.
F. If an octopus loses five of its legs, it would have __ left.

Encyclopedia fun

Name That Animal!

On the same piece of paper, write the name of each animal pictured here.

What do the first letters of those four animal names spell? Can you find a picture of that animal in the book?

What Doesn't Belong Here?

On a separate piece of paper, write down the names of the pictures you see below. Then circle the name of the picture that does not belong with the other three. Do you know why it's different?

Encyclopedia fun

What Am I?

There are eight pictures beside letters here, and there are six descriptions beside numbers below them. On a separate piece of paper, write down the numbers **1** through **6**. Then write next to each number the correct letter of the picture it describes.

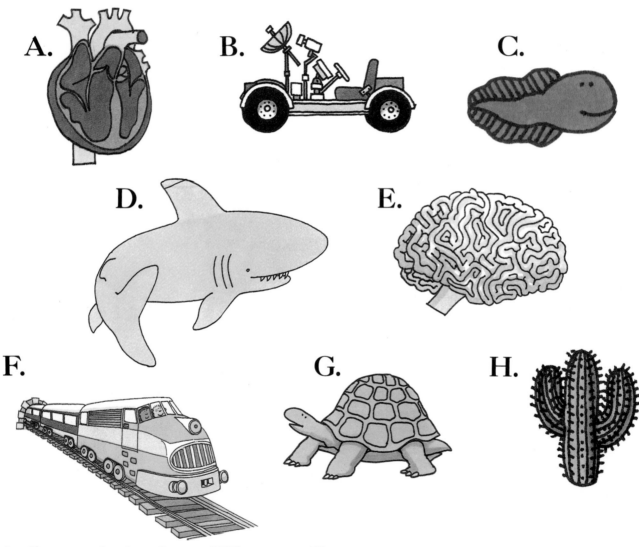

A.   B.   C.

D.   E.

F.   G.   H.

1. I am a baby frog. What am I?
2. I have very sharp teeth. What am I?
3. I tell the rest of your body what to do. What am I?
4. I often live in hot, dry places called deserts. What am I?
5. I can carry a lot of passengers all at the same time. What am I?
6. I like to sleep through the cold winter months. What am I?

ANSWERS

Wheels of Fortune

The four wheeled vehicles are *motorcycle, car, moon buggy,* and *train.* The International Morse code message reads: "It is out of this world." The only wheeled vehicle shown that is used "out of this world" is the moon buggy. It has the money.

Play by the Numbers

A. 8   D. 5
B. 3   E. 9
C. 12   F. 3

Name That Animal!

In order, they are *crocodile, rabbit, ostrich,* and *whale.* The first letters of those four words spell *crow,* pictured in the "More Animals" section.

What Doesn't Belong Here?

Concorde, Orville Wright's airplane, Pteranodon, helicopter
The Pteranodon doesn't belong here because it's a flying animal, not a flying machine like the other three.

pyramid, tent in the desert, mud hut, three-story house
The pyramid doesn't belong here because it's a place for the dead, not the living.

beetle and bee, spider, ants, butterfly
The spider doesn't belong here because it's not an insect, which the others are.

What Am I?

1. C   4. H
2. D   5. F
3. E   6. G

Index